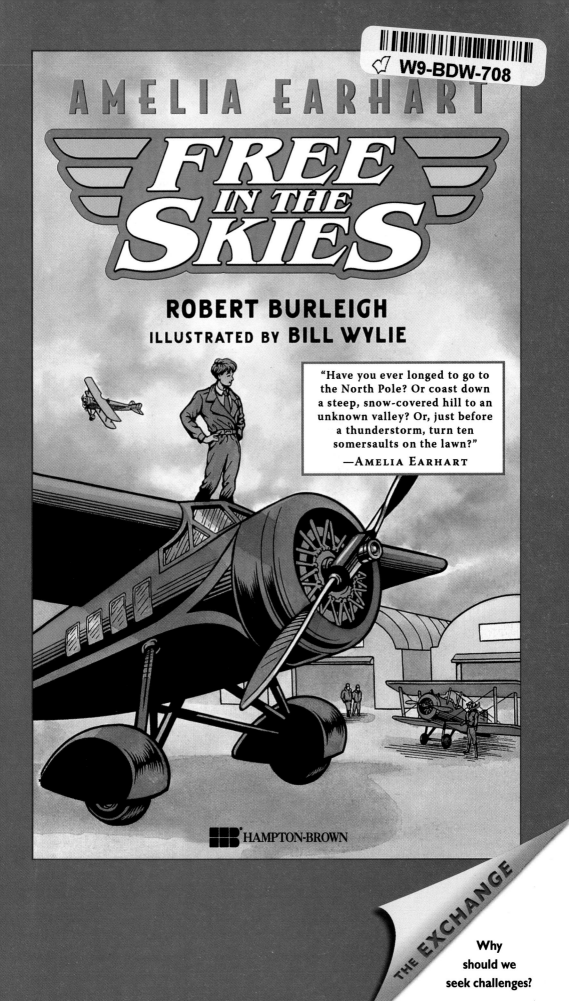

AMELIA EARHART

FREE IN THE SKIES

ROBERT BURLEIGH
ILLUSTRATED BY BILL WYLIE

"Have you ever longed to go to the North Pole? Or coast down a steep, snow-covered hill to an unknown valley? Or, just before a thunderstorm, turn ten somersaults on the lawn?"
—AMELIA EARHART

HAMPTON-BROWN

THE EXCHANGE

Why should we seek challenges?

For Kate Myers Purdum
(and Dee Dee and Todd, too)
—R.B.

To Yuko, with love
—B.W.

Amelia Earhart Free in the Skies by Robert Burleigh,
illustrated by Bill Wylie. Text copyright © 2003 by
Robert Burleigh. Illustrations copyright © 2003 by
Bill Wylie. Published by arrangement with Harcourt, Inc.

Introductions, questions, on-page glossaries,
The Exchange © Hampton-Brown.

Hampton-Brown
P.O. Box 223220
Carmel, California 93922
800-333-3510
www.hampton-brown.com

Printed in the United States of America

ISBN 0-7362-2818-7

05 06 07 08 09 10 11 12 13 14 10 9 8 7 6 5 4 3 2 1

AIRFIELD area where planes are kept

GREAT a lot of

HARDLY not

TAKE A RIDE ride in an airplane

ARRANGE THAT make that happen

KIDDING joking

GIVE IT THE GUN! Let's go!

AND TO THINK I can't believe

HOW WRONG CAN YOU BE? I was wrong!

FREER more free

AT HOME comfortable; not scared

HEADING RIGHT TOWARD going to hit

KID'S GONNA BUST HER NOGGIN is going to
break her head

WIDE-EYED AMELIA SPIES Amelia is excited because she sees

IT'S ONLY A RECIPE FOR LOSING YOUR LUNCH it will make you sick; throw up

LOADS a lot

GET READY, GET SET I'm ready

EUREKA! Yes! Wow!

BEFORE YOU MOVE ON...

1. **Graphic Aids** The words in the book are inside three different shapes. What does each shape mean?

2. **Flashback** Look at pages 6–9. How can you tell that this part of the story happens earlier in Amelia's life?

LOOK AHEAD Read to page 15 to find out how Amelia learns to fly.

WAKING UP TO THE WONDERS OF FLIGHT learning that
flying is exciting

MAKING A LOOP going in a circle; going upside down

"LOOPY" crazy

DEVELOPED EVEN FURTHER made to fly better

YOU'RE IN TROUBLE, YANK. I'm going to fight you,
American.

TAKE OFF leave

THE GOING RATE IS You will have to pay me

MUSS UP YOUR OUTFIT A LITTLE mess up your clothes

DUDE AVIATRIX person who just dresses like a pilot but
doesn't fly

YOU'RE A NATURAL, GIRL. You seem like you've been flying all your life, Amelia.

KEEP IT ON TARGET keep the plane going in the right direction

IN ONE PIECE without having an accident

KEEPS continues

GRADUALLY, AMELIA TAKES ON THE LOOK OF AN EXPERIENCED AVIATOR. SHE BEGINS TO WEAR PANTS AT ALL TIMES RATHER THAN DRESSES.

THE TRUTH IS, I JUST FEEL REALLY GOOD— NOTHING ELSE.

WISH I HAD THIS GAL'S GUTS.

SHORT HAIR IS THE BOLD NEW STYLE OF THE 1920S, SO SHE TRIMS HER ONCE-LONG LOCKS, TOO.

I DON'T WANT MOM TO GET TOO FLUSTERED OVER THIS—

"—SO I'LL DO IT AN INCH AT A TIME!"

WISH I HAD THIS GAL'S GUTS. I wish I could be as brave as Amelia.

TAKES ON THE LOOK OF starts to look like

ONCE-LONG LOCKS long hair

BEFORE YOU MOVE ON...

1. **Details** Look at pages 12–15. How does Amelia learn how to fly?

2. **Inference** Reread pages 10 and 12. How do people feel about airplanes and pilots?

LOOK AHEAD Read pages 16–20 to see how America feels about flying.

AN OPEN-AIR COCKPIT a plane without a roof over the pilot's seat

THE THEN-ASTONISHING ALTITUDE a very high height for the time

TAKE UP RESIDENCE will live

FLY SOLO fly an airplane alone

HIGH-PROFILE important and famous

MAPPING OUT thinking of

TRANSATLANTIC WOMAN PILOT woman who flies across the Atlantic Ocean

SURFACES is talked about

GET THIS SHOW ON THE ROAD—OR IN THE AIR start working

THE QUESTIONS COME THICK AND FAST.

ARE YOU BRAVE ENOUGH TO FLY THE ATLANTIC?

IN THE EVENT OF A DISASTER, WILL YOU RELEASE PUTNAM'S COMPANY FROM ALL RESPONSIBILITY?

IT'S UNCANNY. SHE *DOES* LOOK AS IF SHE COULD BE LINDBERGH'S SISTER!

I ALSO HOPE YOU UNDERSTAND THAT YOU *WON'T* BE AT THE CONTROLS. WE'RE USING AN EXPERIENCED MAN FOR THAT.

THE INTERVIEWERS REMIND AMELIA THAT 14 PEOPLE— INCLUDING 3 WOMEN—HAVE DIED IN ATTEMPTS TO CROSS THE ATLANTIC SINCE LINDBERGH'S SUCCESSFUL FLIGHT.

THE ATLANTIC over the Atlantic Ocean

RELEASE PUTNAM'S COMPANY FROM ALL RESPONSIBILITY agree to not make Putnam pay money if something goes wrong

BE AT THE CONTROLS fly the airplane

19

HESITATES waits and thinks before she answers
ACCEPT will do it

BEFORE YOU MOVE ON...

1. **Cause and Effect** After Lindbergh's flight, how does America feel about flying?

2. **Inference** Reread page 20. Why does Amelia hesitate before she accepts Putnam's offer?

LOOK AHEAD Read pages 21–29 to find out how Amelia's "great adventure" changes her life.

"CAPTAIN" person in charge

LURCHES suddenly goes

DISEMBARK get out of the airplane

REFUELING getting more fuel, or gas

KEEP YOUR FINGERS CROSSED. I hope the flight goes well.

THAT GIRL'S GOT SPUNK. Amelia is brave and full of energy.

KEEPS THE PLANE'S LOG writes about where the plane goes
and what they see

SIGHTS THE SHORES sees the beach

BEATS ME, MATE. I don't know, friend.

GIVE CREDIT WHERE IT'S DUE talk to the people who did the work

I COULD HAVE BEEN A SHEEP FOR ALL THE HELP I WAS I didn't do any work; I didn't matter

DESPITE HER CONTINUING OBJECTIONS, AMELIA IS HAILED AS A HEROINE EVERYWHERE.

BACK IN THE UNITED STATES, SHE IS PRAISED IN THE PRESS, INVITED TO MEET FAMOUS PEOPLE, HIGHLIGHTED IN NEWSREELS, AND CELEBRATED IN PARADE AFTER PARADE!

THREE CHEERS FOR LADY LINDY!

LADY LINDY? THE PILOT DIDN'T EVEN LET ME TOUCH THE CONTROLS—THOUGH I'VE HAD NEARLY FIVE HUNDRED HOURS OF SOLO FLYING!

MY SO-CALLED FAME IS BASED ON NOTHING BUT MERE CHANCE.

CHANCE, MY DEAR AMELIA, IS ANOTHER WORD FOR FATE. YOU'RE AMELIA EARHART THE FAMOUS FLIER NOW, LIKE IT OR NOT.

DESPITE HER CONTINUING OBJECTIONS Even though she doesn't like it

HAILED AS A HEROINE called a female hero

MY SO-CALLED FAME IS BASED ON NOTHING BUT MERE CHANCE. I'm only famous because I was lucky.

25

ENDORSE PRODUCTS AND DELIVER LECTURES help sell
products and give speeches

AVIATION everything relating to airplanes and flying

MEANS OF way to

WEARISOME tiring

JOAN OF ARC female hero who works hard for what she
believes in

FOUND form, create

MAKES IT finishes the race

CONVENTIONAL regular, normal

ON THE WAY while she is flying

BEFORE YOU MOVE ON...

1. **Cause and Effect** How does Amelia's life change because of the Friendship flight?

2. **Summarize** People treat Amelia differently than they treat male pilots. What does she do about this?

LOOK AHEAD Read pages 30–37 to find out about Amelia's solo flight across the Atlantic Ocean.

TURN FICTION INTO FACT really do what people think I did

MORE THAN JUST CARGO flying the plane instead of just sitting in it

IS THIS IT? Will Amelia be able to do it?

READYING HERSELF getting ready

DOUBTS FILL HER MIND she starts to feel afraid

YOU BET, AMELIA. I'm sure you can, Amelia.

TO THE DAY OF after

YOU'LL HEAR FROM ME I'll talk to you again

SO LONG. Good-bye.

LINGERS stays in the sky for a moment
ICEBERGS large pieces of ice that are floating in the ocean

BUT OUT OF NOWHERE—SIGNS OF TROUBLE.

THE ALTIMETER—THE INSTRUMENT THAT MEASURES A PLANE'S ALTITUDE—FLIES CRAZILY OUT OF WHACK.

FSSSSSS

NEXT, A SMALL BLUE FLAME EMERGES FROM THE ENGINE'S EXHAUST.

AHEAD, A BLACK CUMULUS CLOUD GATHERS LIKE A GIANT FIST.

I KNEW IT WAS TOO GOOD TO BE TRUE! BUT THERE'S NO TURNING BACK NOW. IT'S ALL . . . OR NOTHING.

SIGNS OF TROUBLE bad things start to happen

FLIES CRAZILY OUT OF WHACK stops working; shows wrong information

IT'S ALL . . . OR NOTHING. I have to fly or crash.

CLIMB fly

TAKE THIS ALL THE WAY TO THE TOP fly above the storm,
over the clouds

PANIC! Amelia is scared!

EASY DOES IT, AMELIA. I'm going to be calm and careful.

EVERY LAST IOTA all

SHE REGAINS CONTROL OF THE PLANE!

REGAINS CONTROL gets control again

UNCERTAIN OF HER ALTITUDE NOW, SHE MUST CAREFULLY FLY LOW ENOUGH TO KEEP THE WINGS FREE OF ICE—

—BUT HIGH ENOUGH TO AVOID THE TREACHEROUS, FOGBOUND SEA.

TO KEEP THE WINGS FREE OF ICE so that she will not get ice on the wings

BEFORE YOU MOVE ON...

1. **Problem and Solution** What goes wrong on the solo flight? How does Amelia respond?

2. **Context Clues** Reread page 37. *TREACHEROUS* means *dangerous*. How does the picture help you understand that word?

LOOK AHEAD Read pages 38–45. Will Amelia land safely? How will she feel?

INTENSE CONCENTRATION ON thinking only about

CLOUD CREVICES spaces between the clouds

FOR SORE EYES that I am happy to see

SIGHTS A LEVEL PASTURE sees some flat farm land

DESCEND come down from the sky

BESSIES cows

IT'S A SHE It's a woman pilot

FARAWAY AMERICA America, which is very far away

PRAY TELL please tell me
RUNS OFF TO SUMMON goes to tell

ALL MY LIFE! I've been preparing to do this since
I was a child!

FLIGHT flying and pilots

A LEGEND someone who people would remember, talk about, and respect

SHE WAS ALSO A STRONG EARLY ADVOCATE FOR THE IMPORTANCE OF AVIATION, AND SHE ALWAYS SPOKE UP FOR THE RIGHTS OF WOMEN TO PARTICIPATE IN AVIATION—AND OTHER ACTIVITIES—ON AN EQUAL FOOTING WITH MEN.

THE FIRST WOMAN TO CROSS THE ATLANTIC BY PLANE AND THE FIRST WOMAN TO FLY SOLO ACROSS THE ATLANTIC, AMELIA ALSO SET OTHER RECORDS.

THEY INCLUDE THE FASTEST TRANSCONTINENTAL FLIGHT (AT THAT TIME) BY A WOMAN, THE FIRST PERSON TO FLY FROM HAWAII TO CALIFORNIA, AND THE FIRST PERSON TO FLY SOLO FROM LOS ANGELES TO MEXICO.

IN 1937, EARHART, ACCOMPANIED BY A NAVIGATOR, ATTEMPTED TO FLY AROUND THE WORLD AT THE EQUATOR. STARTING FROM THE UNITED STATES AND FLYING EASTWARD, THEY COMPLETED TWENTY-TWO THOUSAND MILES.

BUT ON THE LAST LEG OF THEIR JOURNEY, WHILE ATTEMPTING TO REACH A TINY PACIFIC ISLAND TO REFUEL, THE PLANE DISAPPEARED.

DESPITE A MASSIVE SEARCH, NEITHER THE PLANE NOR THE AVIATORS WERE EVER FOUND.

MANY STORIES HAVE ARISEN ABOUT WHAT REALLY HAPPENED TO AMELIA, BUT MOST PEOPLE NOW AGREE THAT THE PLANE RAN OUT OF FUEL AND CRASHED INTO THE PACIFIC OCEAN, KILLING BOTH MEMBERS OF THE CREW.

BEFORE YOU MOVE ON...

1. **Flashback** Look at pages 42–43. Use the pictures to tell what Amelia is thinking about.

2. **Main Idea and Details** Why is Amelia Earhart an important person in U.S. history?

ADVOCATE supporter

ACCOMPANIED BY A NAVIGATOR with someone to help with directions

LAST LEG final part

MANY STORIES HAVE ARISEN People tell many different stories

Written by ROBERT BURLEIGH

Illustrated by BILL WYLIE